Financially Free at Last

Revolutionary Models of Wealth Ownership

Table of Contents

An investment in knowledge pays the best interest.

— Benjamin Franklin

Chapter 1. Introduction

Unlock the shackles of traditional financial models and step into financial freedom! Our Special Report, "Financially Free at Last: Revolutionary Models of Wealth Ownership," will guide you through an exciting exploration of innovative wealth acquisition strategies. This invigorating journey anticipates your financial liberation, introducing uniquely transformative models hitherto unknown to mainstream economics. Not bogged down by overly technical jargon, our report is designed to make these revolutionary concepts accessible and exciting for everyone. Whether you're an experienced investor looking for fresh perspectives or just starting your journey to financial security, this special report promises to be an enlightening read that could propel you into a world of economic independence you never thought possible. Get ready to rewrite your financial destiny!

Chapter 2. Understanding Your Current Economic Position

The initial leg of our journey to financial independence begins with a comprehensive understanding of our present financial standing. It's a critical but often overlooked aspect that involves taking a candid look at one's economic status, highlighting both strengths and weaknesses. In exploring this concept, we'll tackle two placeholder concepts: income and expenditure analysis, and net worth determination.

2.1. Income and Expenditure Analysis

If you view your finances as a business, your income and expenses are the equivalent of revenue and costs. The beginning of the mapping of your financial self is a careful perusal of your income and expenses. A detailed income and expenditure analysis helps you understand how much you earn and where your money goes.

Firstly, to calculate your total income, you need to consider all revenue sources, not just your salary. This may include interest on savings, dividends from shares, rent from property, and any side hustles. All these diverse income streams contribute to your total revenue and should be taken into account.

Your expenditure, on the other hand, includes all fixed and variable payments made by you. Analyzing your spending habits, you can categorize your expenses into essentials (such as rent, groceries, and utilities) and discretionary spending (like entertainment, dining out, and shopping). The aim is to highlight where your money is going and identify areas where you can minimize expenses.

Recording these figures in a spreadsheet can help visualize your income versus expenditure. It assists in finding patterns, identifying saving opportunities, and planning ahead to boost your total income and reduce unnecessary outlays. However, simply performing this exercise is not enough. Committing to regular reviews and revisions, typically on a monthly basis, will ensure that the analysis remains relevant to your current situation and adjusts for any changes in income or expenditure.

2.2. Determination of Net Worth

After understanding your income and expenses, it's time to determine your current net worth. In a nutshell, your net worth is a tangible representation of your current financial position. It is the sum total of your assets (things you own of value like property, investments, and cash) minus your liabilities (debts and obligations).

Understanding your net worth presents a wholesome view of your current economic position, rather than just your income or expenses. It plays a crucial role in developing a realistic financial game plan and setting viable economic goals.

To calculate your net worth, start by listing all of your assets. This includes cash and cash equivalents like checking and savings accounts, physical properties like homes and cars, investments like stocks and bonds, retirement accounts like 401Ks or RRSPs, and any personal belongings with significant value like jewelry or art pieces.

Subsequently, list all your liabilities. These could involve credit card debt, mortgages, student loans, car loans, personal loans, taxes due, and any other amounts that you owe. Subtract your liabilities from your assets and the result is your net worth.

Calculating your net worth should not be a one-time task. Your financial situation can change rapidly, influenced by factors such as salary adjustments, property value shifts, investment fluctuations, or changes in your debt level. To keep up to date with your current economic standing, calculate your net worth periodically, every three to six months can be suitable intervals.

Understanding where you stand financially is the cornerstone of any financial plan. It gives you a starting point from which to launch your strategy for achieving financial freedom. It will also help you gauge your progress along the journey. The next chapters will help explore innovative strategies and options to improve your net worth and accelerate your path to financial independence. However, remember the key point - a solid financial plan starts with understanding your current economic position.

Chapter 3. Decoding the Mystery of Wealth

Ultimately, the key to obtaining wealth hinge on our understanding of what wealth truly is. Many misconely comprehend it as an abundance of money or valuable possessions, but the truth can diverge significantly from this preconception.

3.1. The Elements of Wealth

To break down the concept, think of wealth as an equation consisting of several components. The first element is income, brought into your sphere through employment, entrepreneurship, investments, and other endeavours. It's important to recognize that a high income is not synonymous with wealth. It's merely the fuel that can catapult your journey toward building wealth.

The second element is savings. Easy to overlook given its quiet nature, saving is fundamental to the accumulation of wealth. The discipline to consistently set aside a portion of your income, regardless of its size, is a habit shared by many financially successful individuals.

The third component is investments. These constitute the decision to delegate your savings to opportunities that generate a return, thus multiplying your wealth passively.

The final element can be referred to as legacy. This is the enduring aspect of wealth that can be transferred across generations. It includes everything from physical assets to business interests and financial securities. Leaving behind a legacy is often regarded as the pinnacle of wealth creation.

3.2. The Illusion of Money Equals Wealth

In our consumerist society, it's easy to equate money with wealth. However, money is a means to an end, not an end in itself. Money is merely a tool that can be used to acquire goods, services, experiences, and opportunities. It's important to realize that the value of money is dependent upon what it can be exchanged for, i.e., its purchasing power.

As an exercise, consider a scenario where you find yourself stranded on a deserted island. In this situation, a suitcase full of money would be inherently worthless, as there's nothing to exchange it for. Conversely, having ample knowledge about survival techniques would be infinitely more valuable.

Not all assets are created equal, and the potential wealth they embody extends beyond their monetary worth. Knowledge and time, for example, can't be quantified in pounds or dollars, but their worth is undeniably immense. Understanding the real worth of money and other non-tangible assets helps in better comprehending the true essence of wealth.

3.3. Money, Wealth, and Freedom

It is critical to appreciate the distinction between having money and having wealth. Money is temporary and fleeting, easily expended and lost, while wealth is durable and potentially enduring. Wealth is the accumulation of assets that are valuable and cultivate a consistent growth pattern over time.

Wealth has the power to offer you options and freedom. It's the capability to take a spontaneous vacation, support your family in an emergency, or decide on a career shift with minimal financial stress. This aspect of wealth, the potential to provide financial security and freedom, is a central tenet of our understanding and pursuit of wealth.

3.4. Wealth's Intangible Aspects

While there's a strong focus on the material aspects of wealth, such as money and physical possessions, it's key to recognize the intangible aspects as well. Knowledge, confidence, emotional well-being, relationships, and time are all elements of wealth in their own right.

Knowledge, for example, is an extraordinarily valuable form of wealth. The more you know, the more opportunities you can seize. It can't be stolen, lost, or easily depleted. Similarly, time is a non-renewable, precious resource that, when properly used, can lead to immense prosperity.

These intangible aspects of wealth provide a broader perspective on what it truly means to be wealthy. Being wealthy isn't just about having money; it's about achieving a balance in various aspects of life that matter most to you.

3.5. The Everyday Practice of Creating Wealth

Understanding that wealth extends beyond mere money is just the first step. Building wealth takes time, patience, discipline, and effort. Wealth is not an accident; rather, it is the product of deliberate decisions, such as saving consistently, investing wisely, encompassing both tangible and intangible assets in your wealth basket, and having financial resilience in the face of unforeseen circumstances.

The practical steps towards building wealth vary from individual to individual, based on their unique circumstances, goals, and values. However, the core principles of saving and investing, valuing time, and imparting knowledge remain universal. Growing your wealth is a practice that demands daily attention.

Decoding the mystery of wealth, we realize that it is not an elusive concept within the exclusive reach of a privileged few. With the right mindset and practical steps, it can be attained by anyone willing to dedicate their efforts towards achieving it. It is the perpetual journey towards financial freedom and security in the face of an uncertain world.

Chapter 4. Revolutionary Models of Wealth Ownership: An Overview

In the ever-evolving landscape of economic proliferation, wealth acquisition has assumed unrecognizable forms, challenging our ingrained notions of wealth ownership itself. This chapter aims to delve into the heart of these revolutionary models, offering a comprehensive overview that can act as a springboard for your new financial journey.

4.1. Traditional Forms of Wealth Acquisition

Before we venture into the unknown, let's cast a brief glance over the models of wealth acquisition that have dominated our economic discourse thus far. Traditionally, models of wealth acquisition have operated within the boundaries of steady employment and conventional investment. The idea of earning a steady income from a job or several jobs, carefully balancing expenses against earnings, and setting aside a portion of this hard-earned income to invest in inevitably fluctuating markets was once the cornerstone of economic life.

Customers participating in the market economy would typically invest in stocks, bonds, real estate, and other tangibles, navigating a delicate balance between closeness to the marketplace and the risk of loss. While these traditional models offered monetary growth and economic stability, they also placed spirit-crushing limitations on individuals, introducing the persistent fear of a single point of failure if one's job or investments went awry. To truly experience economic freedom, one had to break free from this single-minded pursuit and seek opportunities that offered multiple routes to growth - a mindset shift marking the dawn of revolutionary models of wealth ownership.

4.2. The Revolutionary Shift

The inception of these groundbreaking economic models invited not just an economic but also a paradigmatic shift. This transformation introduced an entirely new dimension to how we perceive, acquire, and possess wealth. Rather than waiting out the market fluxes in hope of high returns or relying on a singular income source, the revolutionary models propose a multi-pronged approach.

Here, wealth is no longer just the gold stacked in your vault or the digits displayed on your screen. Instead, it is a multi-dimensional concept colored by factors like multiple income streams, financial resilience, novel investment ventures (such as cryptocurrencies), shared economies, crowdfunded businesses, and more. The wealth acquisition diversifies, multiplies and even becomes democratised, offering higher resilience and financial security.

4.3. Multiple Income Streams

As the adage goes, don't place all your eggs in one basket. Today's economic environment encourages wealth diversification, urging individuals to explore myriad income-generating activities. It could be a mix of active income from a job or a business, passive income from investments or rentals, or royalty payments for your intellectual property. The possibilities are numerous, and with the right mix, one can unlock unprecedented financial freedom and resilience.

4.4. The Rise of the Digital Economy

The turn of the new century introduced a game-changer in wealth acquisition models - the advent of the digital economy. Cryptocurrencies, digital assets, and blockchain technology have garnered tremendous interest for their potential to revolutionize the financial world. The openness, decentralization, and high potential returns of digital currencies such as Bitcoin and Ethereum have started challenging traditional financial systems. They provide an alternative platform for investment and wealth accumulation, redefining wealth ownership and our perception of what 'counts' as an asset.

4.5. Shared Economies and Crowdfunding

Our generation has also seen a sharp rise in shared economies – a powerful indicator of the changing wealth acquisition landscape. Examples like Uber and Airbnb have redefined the concepts of ownership and income generation. Crowdfunding, another remarkable innovation, allows regular individuals to invest in promising projects or startups and enjoy the returns of successful ventures.

4.6. Economic Resilience

Lastly, these revolutionary models promote economic resilience. Economic uncertainties are a constant facet of our lives. By building multiple income sources, investing in emerging markets, and utilizing novel tactics, one can create a robust financial cushion that can weather any economic storm.

In conclusion, this chapter encapsulates the revolutionary shift towards more empowering and liberating models of wealth ownership and acquisition. The journey ahead will delve into the specifics of these models, making you competent and confident to step into a daring new world of financial freedom.

Chapter 5. Radical Reforms in Traditional Investment

In the evolving landscape of investment strategies, there has been a notable shift away from old-fashioned models to a more dynamic and revolutionary approach. This shift is primarily driven by rapid technological advancements and growing investor awareness and education. Traditional investments have taken a new shape, and radical reforms in them are making waves in financial ecosystems around the world.

5.1. The Rising Influence of Technology

In the post-industrial revolution era, the increasing intersection of technology and finance has led to substantial changes in how investment strategies are formed and executed. First, the digitization of assets, which has allowed investments to become more liquid, diversified, and accessible. Rather than being restricted by geographical boundaries, investors can now buy, sell, and trade securities from across the world at the swipe of a finger, thanks to online trading platforms.

The use of robo-advisors is another prominent example of how automation is reforming traditional investment strategies. These automated platforms use intricate algorithms to manage and balance investment portfolios. Not only do robo-advisors offer a low-cost alternative to traditional financial advisors, but they also grant investors access to sophisticated, data-driven investment strategies that were once reserved for successful hedge funds and major financial institutions.

Another technological innovation reshaping traditional investment models is the use of safety algorithms, designed to reduce the risks associated with investing. These algorithms conduct rigorous real-time checks on investment options to flag potential threats - offering an added layer of protection to investors.

5.2. Democratization of Investment Strategies

Historically, investment opportunities were often reserved for the elite or those with vast resources. However, recent reforms have led to a democratization of investments. Today, investment opportunities are no longer exclusive. Accessing and managing investments have become more user-friendly, allowing people from all walks of life to participate in wealth creation.

Crowdfunding platforms, for instance, have made it possible for ordinary individuals to invest in private companies, startups, and real estate projects with relatively small sums of money. Alternatively, apps for investing in stock and bond markets have brought Wall Street to Main Street, enabling every individual with a smartphone and internet connection to invest directly in the market – an unprecedented shift.

5.3. Sustainable and Ethical Investing

Environmental, social, and governance (ESG) criteria have grown immensely popular among modern investors. ESG investing, also known as sustainable or ethical investing, involves considering the above factors, along with traditional financial metrics, to guide investment decisions.

ESG investing aims to generate long-term competitive returns while creating a positive societal impact. An increasing number of consumers are making purchase decisions based on ethical considerations, which has led many businesses to overhaul their practices. Traders and financiers have followed suit, with ESG factors playing an increasingly important role in investment decision making.

The push for ethical investment options has also been fueled by an increasing awareness about global socio-environmental challenges such as climate change, human rights issues, and unethical corporate behavior. Investors are increasingly considering these factors when making decisions about where to put their money.

5.4. Embracing Globalization in Investment

Globalization has changed the face of investing by eliminating borders and promoting international trade. Greater access to global markets has transformed the investment process. With the click of a button, even small-scale investors can spread their capital across diverse international markets, helping them minimize risk and boost potential returns through increased diversification.

Moreover, emerging markets present an enticing investment opportunity, offering high growth rates compared to mature economies. While these markets pose substantial risk, they can offer significant returns, making them a worthwhile consideration for risk-tolerant investors.

In conclusion, the radical reforms in traditional investment is a testament to the rapid shifts in societal norms and technological advancements. The age-old ways of investing are being challenged, paving the way for a more inclusive, ethical, and diversified investment landscape. These changes are likely to continue as technology advances and the definition of 'investor' broadens. In a world changing at a faster pace than ever before, keeping abreast of these radical reforms and aligning them with your investment strategy can be the key to successful wealth creation.

Chapter 6. Crowdfunding and Peer-to-Peer Lending: The New Investment Frontiers

The contemporary world is more interconnected than ever before, initiated by the advent of internet revolution. In this rapidly evolving landscape, emerging models have started challenging the status quo in various aspects of our lives. The domain of finance proves no exception, with crowdfunding and peer-to-peer lending platforms giving the conventional financial systems a solid run for their money.

6.1. The Rise of Crowdfunding and its Implications

Crowdfunding is a relatively young, yet highly influential, player in the world's financial game, having only come into the limelight in the last decade or so. This revolutionary approach to raising capital relies on small contributions from a large number of individuals, aggregating these funds to support a specific project, business, or cause. It's an entirely new mechanism for nurturing and proliferating innovative ideas, entrepreneurial ventures, and socially conscientious initiatives.

Crowdfunding is unique due to its reliance on the power of collective effort. This communal aspect extends beyond the financial contributions and includes sharing of knowledge, skills, network, and time. Its potency lies in its capacity to provide multidimensional support to the fundraiser, amplifying the chances of success.

Crowdfunding platforms are incredibly diverse in nature. Some of the common types include reward-based crowdfunding (funders receive a reward or perk in return for their contribution), equity crowdfunding (funders receive a stake or shares in the venture they fund), and donation-based crowdfunding (funders contribute without expecting anything tangible in return).

The implications of crowdfunding are multifaceted and profound. First, crowdfunding erases geographical barriers to raising capital, making it possible for ideas to flourish regardless of their origin. Second, it increases the overall access to funds, particularly for undertakings that would struggle to secure capital using conventional financial systems. Third, it democratizes the investment process by allowing anyone with an internet connection to become an investor.

6.2. Peer-to-Peer Lending: Unveiling a New Horizon in Accessible Finance

Yet another groundbreaking trend in the modern financial landscape is the rise of peer-to-peer lending (P2P lending). Rooted in the primary principle of two-way direct interaction, it eliminates the need for a conventional financial institution as an intermediary. Instead, it creates a digital marketplace where potential lenders and borrowers can transact directly. This direct interaction not only reduces costs by cutting down on the layers of intermediaries but also leads to greater transparency and improves the speed of lending.

There are three main types of P2P lending: consumer loans, business loans, and bespoke loans, each aligning with a specific lending scenario. In consumer loans, individuals loan money for personal use such as purchasing a car, funding an education, or consolidating debt. Business loans involve lending money to businesses for operational or growth purposes, while bespoke loans are tailored to cater to unique situations or needs.

One of the chief strengths of P2P lending is that it opens up opportunities for a large number of individuals and small businesses who have previously been deemed unworthy of credit by traditional banks. By using big data and machine learning, P2P lending platforms can assess credit risk more effectively and provide unsecured loans at competitive interest rates on both ends - the lender and the borrower.

6.3. The Combined Force of Crowdfunding and Peer-to-Peer Lending

Crowdfunding and P2P lending have jointly spearheaded a financial metamorphosis that is still unfolding. These models have transformed the financial decision-making process, making it more transparent, inclusive, and diversified. They've broadened the notion of 'investing' to include not just the wealthy elite but also individuals who want to contribute small amounts towards causes they believe in.

The dynamic and novel nature of these models also means that they're continuously evolving with numerous cutting-edge variations, hybrid models, and subsets taking shape. They continue to push boundaries and create a ripple of change in how we perceive the world of investing, raising capital, and engaging with finance at large.

Moreover, as these models gain regulatory recognition, their potential to challenge the conventional financial powerhouses becomes increasingly apparent. They signify a shift toward decentralization of power, the democratization of wealth, and an overall more inclusive financial system.

6.4. Conclusion: The Transcendent Potential of Crowdfunding and Peer-to-Peer Lending

In conclusion, the advent of crowdfunding and peer-to-peer lending marks a turning point in the history of financial models. Their democratizing effects and the propensity to empower individuals make them quintessential agents of change in the financial world. Although they pose challenges for regulatory bodies, as happens when any paradigm shift occurs, this should not detract from their transformative potential. As we continue the onward march towards an even more connected world, these revolutionary models hold the promise for a more inclusive, financially empowered global community.

Chapter 7. The Onset of Cryptocurrency and Digital Assets

In the vast ecosystem of progressive financial models, a new entrant is creating quite a stir. This is no ordinary player but a revolutionary one that holds the potential to redefine the way we perceive and transact wealth: the world of Cryptocurrency and Digital Assets. Although seemingly complex and relatively recent, understanding these concepts is vital in today's digital era. Let us sail through this fascinating seascape together.

7.1. The Dawn of Digital Assets

At the core of the digital revolution are digital assets. An asset is a valuable item owned by an individual or corporate body. The traditional views of assets are physical items such as real estate, vehicles, or gold. Digital assets, however, are a radical shift from this. These are non-tangible valuables that exist solely in a digital environment. Ranging from digital currencies like Bitcoin to intellectual properties like digital music or electronic books, digital assets have made a significant stand in the online world.

Understanding digital assets is to perceiving the paradigms of the internet economy. For instance, a software application developed by a programmer is a digital asset that can be licensed to multiple users, generating a continuous stream of income. Similarly, domain names, mobile applications, and social media profiles are all examples of digital assets that hold potential economic value in today's digital age.

7.2. Digital Assets: Powering Modern Economies

While it is easy to grasp that an entity of value, digital or physical, can be classified as an asset, the economic implications of digital assets are far more complex. For any transaction or trade to occur, both parties must mutually agree on the value of the traded goods or services. This rudimentary principle of commerce holds even in the digital realm. A blog, for instance, may be a digital asset for a writer. But it obtains tangible value when readers visit, generating advertisement revenue.

The power of digital assets in modern economies is profound. In a traditional model, the transaction of a physical item entails the surrender of its ownership. Digital assets, on the other hand, can be cloned without altering the original copy, facilitating multiple ownership estates across different geographies. This multi-fold increase in value proposition, combined with the ease and speed of digital transactions, has fueled the proliferation of digital assets across the globe.

7.3. Cryptocurrency: The Radical Offspring of Digital Wealth

Cryptocurrency, a powerful derivative of digital assets, was conceptualized with a vision. It aimed to replace traditional fiat currencies and create a decentralized financial ecosystem devoid of any central authority. Bitcoin, the pioneer, set the stage for the cryptocurrency surge with its introduction in 2009.

Cryptocurrencies exist as digital or virtual currencies that utilize cryptography for securing transactions. Unlike traditional financial systems governed by central banks, cryptocurrencies operate over decentralized networks based on blockchain technology. This ingenious network system is essentially a public ledger that verifies and records each transaction made. Some well-known cryptocurrencies aside from Bitcoin include Ethereum, Ripple, and Litecoin.

7.4. Understanding Blockchain: The Backbone of Cryptocurrencies

Blockchain technology is to cryptocurrency what a robust engine is to a high-performance supercar. It is an ingenious solution that not only powers cryptocurrencies but also ensures their security and transparency. A blockchain is a widespread network of computers or nodes that collectively maintain a decentralized database of ownership. Once data enters this chain, it is nearly impossible to modify, providing an unparalleled degree of security to cryptocurrency transactions.

The information within a blockchain is sorted into blocks, which are essentially bundles of data that are linked or 'chained' together using complex mathematical algorithms. This continuous linking of blocks forms the 'chain' and hence the name - blockchain. When a new transaction occurs, it is added to the end of this chain, allowing a transparent trail of past transactions.

7.5. Embracing Cryptocurrency: The Rewards and Risks

Cryptocurrency, much like the sweeping revolution it represents, brings a host of rewards. The decentralized nature of this digital currency ensures minimal transactional fees, as no intermediaries are required. Additionally, its universal acceptability bypasses the hassle of currency conversion during international transactions. Its data transparency, coupled with transaction speeds that conventional banking methods can hardly match, adds to its allure. Furthermore, cryptocurrencies offer an extensive field for investment and speculation, carrying the promise of high returns.

However, the world of cryptocurrencies is not without its risks. The market's highly volatile nature can lead to substantial losses in a very short duration. This volatility, coupled with regulatory uncertainties in many countries, often stirs skepticism among potential users and investors. Additionally, while blockchain technology ensures the security of transactions and the integrity of data, digital wallets storing these cryptocurrencies could be vulnerable to cyber-attacks.

To actively partake in the world of digital assets and cryptocurrencies, one must thoroughly evaluate these potential rewards and risks. It's crucial to tread this path with knowledge, preparedness, and a fair bit of caution. After all, being financially free also means being financially responsible. And with that, our journey through the fascinating landscape of digital currencies and assets comes to an end, hopefully leaving you better equipped and filled with anticipation for the chapters to come.

Chapter 8. Shared Economies: A Peek into the Future

In an era where individual ownership loses its dominance to collective use and participation, the shared economy is swiftly emerging as a major force in the quest for financial freedom. As we tilt our gaze towards tomorrow, the narrative of economics undergoes this radical transformation, underpinning the heart of our chapter.

8.1. An Introduction to the Shared Economies

Imagine for a moment, the global exchange of goods, services, even space, no longer limited by traditional constraints of ownership, but facilitated by digital platforms that tap into the collective capacity of communities. Welcome to the realm of shared economies. Operating under the maxim, "Access over Ownership," shared economies are built on the principle of utilizing underused assets to derive value and build solid income streams.

With roots in various culturally ingrained practices such as communal farmlands or shared neighborhood resources, the concept of shared economies has undergone a contemporary digital rebirth. Aided by technological advancements and catalyzed by the pervasive use of the internet, we now witness phenomenally successful enterprises like Airbnb, Uber, and TaskRabbit embodying the shared economy model.

8.2. Unraveling How Shared Economies Function

So, how exactly do these shared economies function? Let's decipher this novel process. These business models typically rely on a digital intermediary— a platform, connecting potential service providers with consumers. In this synergistic ecosystem, providers are commonly everyday individuals who are willing to rent out or share their underutilized assets, such as a spare room (Airbnb), a car (Uber), or their time and skills (TaskRabbit).

Consequently, you as an individual no longer have to purchase assets that you need sporadically. Instead, you can now access these resources as and when needed via these platforms, avoiding the considerable cost and hassle of ownership.

For the providers, it creates unique opportunities to monetize otherwise latent assets, thereby generating additional income, a prospect that gels seamlessly with our chase for financial independence.

8.3. The Financial Implications of Shared Economies

When we dive into the financial implications of shared economies, the impact is multifaceted. For starters, by partaking in shared economies, individuals can maneuver through periods of economic fluctuation with increased resilience. The ability to generate income through sharing underutilized resources can offer a financial buffer in uncertain times, a critical dimension of economic self-sustenance.

Additionally, shared economies democratize wealth by redistributing income opportunities. By creating micro-entrepreneurs, they break down larger monopolies, distributing economic welfare more evenly within society.

Yet, shared economies also pose challenges. Regulatory frictions, liability concerns, and apprehensions around trust and quality often lurk around these business models. It becomes imperative then for existing and aspiring participants to stay abreast of changing legal landscapes and shifting societal attitudes towards shared economies.

8.4. Preparing for a Shared Economy Future

As we direct our thoughts towards embracing a shared economy future, a few key strategies come into sharp focus. At an individual level, it is crucial to identify latent resources, both tangible and intangible, that can be shared. From your car to your crafting skills, each is a potential source of income.

On a larger scale, we need collaborative legal frameworks that support and regulate the shared economy, protecting the interests of all parties involved. Maintaining and enhancing the user experience, trust, and quality will also be critical to sustainable growth in this sector.

In conclusion, the shared economy is a revolutionary model that disrupts traditional norms of ownership, thereby creating multiple streams of income, and bestows upon us a peek into the future of the economic world. In our ongoing journey towards financial freedom, adapting, and thriving in this shared economy can pave the path to economic independence and resilience. This chapter has merely skimmed the surface of the iceberg that is shared economies—a concept set to redefine our relationship with wealth, property, and each other as we sail into the future.

Chapter 9. Building & Sustaining Multiple Sources of Income

Before embarking on an enlightening journey of creating and sustaining multiple streams of income, it is crucial to delve into an understanding of its importance. Warren Buffet, one of the most successful investors of all time, once asserted, "Do not rely on a single income. Make investments to create a second source."

9.1. Understanding the Importance of Multiple Sources of Income

Earning income from numerous resources can certainly accelerate your movement towards financial freedom. It is akin to casting a wider net into the sea of opportunities. By creating multiple income streams, you are diversifying the ways you earn, which can be especially beneficial during periods of economic uncertainties or market downturns. When one income source is impacted, the others can keep you financially afloat.

9.2. Diversification: Not Putting All Your Eggs in One Basket

The idea behind diversification is relatively simple and straightforward. It's based on the inherent uncertainty of the future. As we don't know what the future holds, it's prudent to spread the risk by having multiple income sources. This way, if one investment performs poorly or one income stream dries up, the negative impact on your entire portfolio is limited.

9.3. Identifying Viable Sources of Additional Income

When it comes to determining additional income sources, there's no 'one-size-fits-all' approach. The options are vast and depend on different factors such as your interests, skills, time commitment, risk tolerance, and initial investment. Some popular ways to establish multiple income streams include real estate investments, stock market investments, starting a side business, freelance work, or turning a hobby into a profitable venture. Think about the resources at your disposal, and consider how they could be leveraged to create additional income.

9.4. From Idea to Implementation: Setting Up Your Multiple Income Streams

Once you've identified a potential source of additional income, the next step is to get it off the ground. This usually involves a well-thought-out plan detailing the implementation strategy, time and financial commitment, potential hurdles, and contingency plans. It's also crucial to understand the tax implications of your additional income sources.

9.5. Sustaining Your Multiple Sources of Income

Just as important as establishing your multiple income streams, is the task of maintaining them. This will require continuous active management, monitoring, and adapting to ever-changing economic conditions and market trends. Depending on your chosen income source, this might involve staying updated with market trends, continuously enhancing your skills, or innovatively marketing your product or service.

9.6. Paving the Way Towards Financial Resilience

In conclusion, building and sustaining multiple sources of income serve as cornerstone components of a robust financial plan. By diversifying your income, you are not only creating a buffer against potential economic downturns but also accelerating your journey towards economic independence. Remember, consistent effort and strategic planning will be your allies on this path. With each additional income source, you are paving a new pathway towards financial resilience.

Ultimately, the aim is not to create a life that is overly consumed with making ends meet, but rather, one that provides an enabling environment for you to enjoy the things you love, while generating a steady income from multiple sources. This chapter, hopefully, leaves you with considerable insights to explore the exciting realm of multiple income streams and to liberally spread your earnings wings.

Chapter 10. Financial Resilience: Preparing for Economic Uncertainties

The pathway to financial freedom is hardly a straight road. It is instead a journey peppered with a series of unpredictable bumps and obstacles. Even the most meticulously crafted routes can be thwarted by the tumultuous waves of the global economy, necessitating a deep understanding of how to prepare for and navigate these roiling seas. The strength of your financial fortitude is indeed determined by your ability to weather these uncertainties. It is this very capacity for economic resilience that is pivotal to your liberation from traditional financial constraints.

10.1. Navigating Economic Uncertainty

There is a common misconception that financial resilience is about accumulating extraordinary amounts of wealth. However, resilience isn't tied to the quantity of wealth amassed, but rather how effectively you're able to manage your resources in the face of uncertainty. By understanding this, you open a door to a new way of thinking about your economic position, underpinned by preparedness rather than simple acquisition.

Facing economic uncertainty is like standing on the shoreline. One never knows if the tide will bring in an unexpected catch or recede, leaving the sand barren. Yet, the fisherman must persist, adjusting his tactics according to the changing tide to survive and thrive, using the art of strategies such as diversification, liquidity management, risk management and innovative trends.

10.2. Diversification: Spreading Your Assets

Diversification is the initial step towards establishing financial resilience. A diversified investment portfolio is an assortment of varied financial assets—stocks, bonds, mutual funds, real estate, and more recently, cryptocurrencies and other digital assets. It dilutes your risk exposure by spreading your investments across multiple categories. By employing this tactic, you can decrease potential losses without severely affecting your potential profits.

10.3. Proper Liquidity Management

Liquidity, or the availability of your assets in cash form, is another critical component of financial resilience. While investments like real estate and bonds may promise impressive returns, they are not immediately accessible or convertible to cash when an economic shock hits. It's, therefore, essential to maintain a sensible balance between short-term, readily accessible assets and long-term, high-return ones. Your cash reserves or 'emergency fund' play an indispensable role in cushioning you against financial shocks.

10.4. Understanding and Managing Business Risks

Risk is intrinsic to business, and an awareness of the various risks—market risk, credit risk, operational risk—can equip you with the armor necessary for combating them. Accurate risk assessment involves deciphering the potential threats that can disrupt your business and devising appropriate strategies to counter these challenges. Risk management isn't just about averting these adversities; it's also about identifying and seizing opportunities that emerge amidst these challenges, turning what may appear as setbacks into stepping stones.

10.5. Keeping Abreast of Innovative Trends

One critical aspect of preparing for economic uncertainties is staying updated with emerging trends and innovative concepts. For instance, monitoring the constant evolution of investment frontiers like peer-to-peer lending and crowdfunding can offer a competitive edge. Similarly, understanding the workings of digital currencies and blockchain technology can open up new avenues for wealth accumulation. Therefore, constant learning and willingness to adapt new strategies is a significant aspect of financial resilience.

10.6. Shaping Your Resilience: Tools and Techniques

Beyond diversification, liquidity management, risk management and arming yourself with knowledge, specific methodologies can further help you shape and strengthen your financial resilience. Tools such as Monte Carlo simulations and other stochastic modeling methods can aid in understanding potential financial scenarios and shaping a resilient investment strategy. Likewise, leveraging financial planning and budgeting tools, investment trackers, and engaging with financial advisers can provide much-needed insights and mentorship.

10.7. Conclusion: Journey Towards Resilience

Whether you are setting sail on your journey towards financial freedom or are a seasoned navigator, resilience is an invaluable asset. True financial freedom isn't merely predicated on the accumulation of wealth, but on the ability to harness that wealth to weather economic uncertainties, adapt, and grow. Remember, by nurturing your financial resilience you are not only bolstering your wealth but also fortifying your route to liberation from the shackles of traditional financial models. So, chart your course with confidence, equipped with the tools, knowledge, and insightful strategies this chapter offers, and discover the resilience within you as you journey towards financial liberation.

Chapter 11. Mapping Your Path Towards Financial Freedom

Navigating the world of finance and personal wealth can be likened to embarking on a journey. Just like mapping your path on a road trip, your route to financial freedom needs to be plotted out, with clear markers showing your goalposts and intermediate milestones. This disruptive approach to understanding financial independence empowers you to take control of your economic destiny, enabling you to plan effectively and anticipate obstacles.

11.1. The Destination: Defining Your Financial Freedom

Your path to financial freedom begins with a clear understanding of what financial freedom means to you. This definition will vary for everyone, influenced by factors such as personal values, current financial situation, long-term goals, and risk tolerance.

For some, financial freedom could mean having enough savings and investments to cover living expenses without working full-time. Others might aspire to a millionaire lifestyle with no debt and the possibility to afford high-end living. There's no 'one-size-fits-all' when it comes to financial freedom. It's important to remember, it's not just about the amount of money you acquire but how you use it to create a life that aligns with your values and aspirations.

11.2. The Roadmap: Setting Your Financial Goals

Once you've defined what financial freedom means to you, the next step is to set your financial goals. These goals should be specific, measurable, achievable, relevant, and time-bound (SMART).

These curated financial objectives might include paying off a specific amount of debt, accumulating a certain amount in savings or investments, creating multiple income streams or establishing a retirement fund. Their relevance lies in their alignment to your long-term vision of economic independence. By setting specific goals, you essentially develop a roadmap that serves as a guide towards financial liberation.

11.3. The Travel Kit: Building Your Financial Skillset

Just like you'd need a compass, map, or GPS for effective navigation on a journey, in the odyssey towards financial freedom, you will need specific tools and skills.

Understanding the basics of personal finance, honing your budgeting skills, becoming adept at investing, and learning about tax implications can significantly enhance your journey. Equipping yourself with in-depth knowledge of various asset classes, financial markets, and investment strategies will provide a solid foundation for your financial journey.

11.4. The Path Less Travelled: Exploring Innovative Wealth Models

While traditional models of wealth acquisition emphasize salary increments, saving, and retirement funds, contemporary models offer more dynamic and accessible pathways to wealth.

These include Crowdfunding, Peer-to-Peer Lending, Cryptocurrencies, and the Sharing Economy. These platforms not only democratize wealth but also accelerate the financial liberation process. By exploring these alternative avenues and incorporating them into your overall financial strategy, you blaze a trail towards financial freedom that's uniquely yours.

11.5. Staying the Course: Navigating Economic Uncertainties

Economic conditions are in a constant state of flux, making it crucial to develop resilience and adaptability on your journey to financial independence. This involves creating a financial safety net, diversifying your investment portfolio, and staying informed about global economic trends.

Preparing for economic uncertainties involves understanding and effectively managing risks. Regular review and adjustment of your financial plan will ensure that you stay on the right track, overcoming financial hurdles and adapting to evolving economic landscapes.

Your journey to financial freedom is a personal and transformative process. By understanding and defining your financial goals, building a robust financial skillset, embracing innovative wealth ownership models, and preparing for economic uncertainties, you can map a path towards financial freedom that it's not only achievable but also aligns perfectly with your unique life aspirations. Embrace your financial power, and remember, as you do this, you're not just building wealth. You're also creating a life of purpose, peace, and choice.